First published in the UK by
HarperCollins Children's Books in 2010
1 3 5 7 9 10 8 6 4 2
ISBN: 978-0-00-735387-3

A CIP catalogue record for this title is available
from the British Library.

The HarperCollins website address is:
www.harpercollins.co.uk

Printed and bound in China

Hello Kitty

Guide to Friendship

HarperCollins *Children's Books*

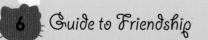

There are so many wonderful things about friendship that I hardly know where to begin! This book is filled with ideas and advice to help you be the best friend you possibly can.

There are lots of suggestions for fun things to do with your friends, ideas for thoughtful gifts to make and advice on staying in touch. You can read my top tips for being a better friend, find out how to start your own club and make a time capsule to preserve your friendship for years to come.

You can never have too many friends and this book will help you make the most of each and every one!

Lots of love,

Hello Kitty
x

Contents

Friendship
Basics

 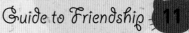

What makes a good friend?

Listening

A true friend will always make time to hear what you have to say.

There are lots of qualities a true friend will have. These are the things I see in my friends, and I hope they see in me, too!

Sharing

Friends should share things without even thinking about it.

Being thoughtful

Friends should try to do nice things for each other, whether that's giving a surprise gift or baking a cake.

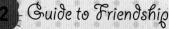

Remembering

Friends should always remember the things that are important to each other... and birthdays, of course!

Cheering up

When you're feeling down, a friend should be able to make you smile again.

Keeping secrets

You have to know you can trust a friend to keep your secrets safe.

Encouraging

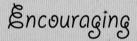

Good friends should make hard things easier to do.

Having fun

If you can't have fun with your friends, who can you have fun with!

Laughing

There's nothing better than having a giggle. Things always seem funnier with friends!

Helping

Whether it's giving advice or tidying up, a good friend will always be ready to help.

Five friends every girl needs

Different friends are good at different things. If you look at your group of buddies I'm sure you'll find the five friends every girl needs in there!

The agony aunt

For times when you need a shoulder to cry on there's only one place to turn – to your agony aunt of course! She'll offer you comfort and support and a great big hug when you need it most.

The helpful friend

When you've got lots to do, your helpful friend will always be there to lend a hand. Whether it's tidying your room or laying the dinner table, she'll happily help you out.

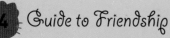

The playful friend

Sometimes you just want to have fun and your playful friend is the perfect person to keep you company! She's full of great ideas for fun things to do and you know you'll always have a good time with her.

The problem solver

When you have a problem and you need advice, turn to your problem-solver friend. She's patient and fair and you know she'll always be honest – even if it isn't always what you want to hear!

The funny friend

If you're feeling a little blue, there's nothing better than a good giggle to lift your spirits. Your funny friend knows how to make you laugh and will cheer you up when you need it most.

Friendship quiz

It's great to have lots of different kinds of friends. Find out what kind you are with this fun quiz.

1. If your friend had a problem would you:
A – Arrange something fun to take her mind off it
B – Give her a big hug and tell her everything will be OK
C – Tell her that you're there for her if she wants to talk

2. What would you give your friend for her birthday?
A – Tickets to an event that you could go to as well
B – Vouchers for her favourite clothes shop
C – Something you've made yourself

3. You're away on holiday. Do you:
A – Email your friends a picture of you enjoying yourself
B – Choose a present to take home for your best friend
C – Send postcards to your closest friends

4. What's your idea of the perfect Friday night?
A – Getting dressed-up and going dancing with lots of friends
B – Baking cookies with your best friend
C – Watching a movie with a few of your friends

5. Your friend is poorly. Do you:
A – Send her a funny text to cheer her up
B – Visit her as soon as she's feeling a bit better

C – Send over her favourite magazine

6. You and your friend want to watch different things on TV. Do you:

A – Decide to do something else instead

B – Record one programme so you can watch it later

C – Watch your friend's programme, you can catch up with yours next week

Mostly As

You are a fun friend! You enjoy being part of a big group and know how to make your friends laugh. There's never a dull moment with you around!

Mostly Bs

You're a great friend to have around! You're a combination of all the friend types on pages 14-15.

Mostly Cs

You are a thoughtful friend! You're kind and caring and know how to make someone feel special. And you'd never forget a birthday!

How to show a friend you care

The little things make a big difference, so don't forget to show your friend how much she means to you.

Make something for her – it will mean so much more than something bought from a shop.

Surprise her with a small present – getting gifts when it isn't your birthday is always lovely!

Download her favourite songs onto one CD – you could even make a cover from photographs and give the album a name!

Send her a card saying why she's your friend.

Buy a copy of her favourite magazine.

Help her with a chore she doesn't like doing – you'll get it done twice as fast!

Let her borrow your favourite top – as long as she promises to look after it!

Hire a movie you know she wants to see and invite her over to watch it. Don't forget the popcorn!

Remember their birthday - plan a surprise party or bake her a cake!

Take her on a picnic – make sure you pack all her favourite things!

Friendship Sayings

"Friendship isn't about who you've known the longest... it's about who came and never left your side."

"A friend is the one who walks in when others walk out."

"A true friend sees the first tear, catches the second and stops the third."

"Anyone can make you smile or cry but it takes a friend to make you smile when you already have tears in your eyes."

"People say best friends are hard to find... that's because the best is already mine!"

"Friends make you laugh a little louder, smile a little wider and live a little better."

"There's a point in every true friendship where friends stop being friends and become sisters."

"A true friend knows you as well as you know yourself."

Hello Kitty's Friends

Rory

Fifi

Joey

Thomas

Jodie

Tracy

Mimmy

Tim and Tammy

Tippy

Things to Do

Fun things to do with friends

Some things are just better when you do them with friends! Choose one of the ideas below and do it today.

Learn a new skill

Trying new things is fun but it can be a little scary to do on your own. With your friends by your side, the sky's the limit! You could practise a language, teach yourselves how to cook or learn how to sew.

Get outside

Organise a walk for you and your friends. You could go to a park and try to spot as many different types of trees as possible, or walk around town looking at the different styles of buildings.

Top tip
Watch your favourite music channel together for dance ideas!

Bake a cake

There's nothing more satisfying than eating something yummy you've made yourself. Bake a batch of fairy cakes and decorate them with icing, hundreds and thousands, chocolate chips... or anything else you fancy! Try to make each one unique.

Make up a dance routine

Choose your favourite song and choreograph a routine. Once it's perfected you can perform it for your friends.

Sing a song

You don't have to have a fancy karaoke machine to belt out a tune! Put on your favourite song and sing along – make sure you have a hairbrush to use as a microphone!

Paint your nails

Doing both hands yourself is a bit tricky so get a friend to help. You could even experiment with simple patterns such as flowers or hearts, or paint your nails half one colour and half another!

Dress up

Try on funny clothes combinations that you would never normally put together. Who can look the silliest?

Create your own magazine

Write the features and cut out cool pictures from other magazines to create your very own magazine.

Friendship games

Some things are just better when you do them with friends! Choose one of the ideas below and do it today.

Pin the bow on Hello Kitty

Draw an outline of my face on a large piece of paper. On a separate piece of paper, draw a bow, carefully cut it out and put a piece of reusable adhesive on the back. Blindfold the first person and gently spin them round five times. Once they have pinned the bow onto the picture, carefully remove it and write their initials in its place. The person who gets the bow nearest to the correct place is the winner.

Top tip
Keep playing the game until someone gets the bow in exactly the right spot.

Who am I?

Everyone writes the name of a famous person on a sticky note and sticks it onto the forehead of someone else – make sure they don't see what it says! Take it in turns to ask questions to try and discover who you are. You can only ask questions that can be answered with a 'yes' or 'no'. The first person to correctly guess who they are is the winner. Keep playing until everyone has guessed who they are.

Top tip
Choose famous people who everyone will know or the game could go on for ages!

Silly stories

Decide who will start this game and give them a piece of paper and a pen. The first person writes the opening paragraph of a story, then folds the piece of paper so only the last line is visible. The next person continues writing the story, then folds the piece of paper so only the last line of their paragraph is showing. Keep going until everyone has written a paragraph. The last person can then unfold the piece of paper and read the story aloud.

Top tip
Try to make your story as silly as possible!

Doughnut line

Buy a ring doughnut for everyone and tie a clean piece of string around each one. Attach the doughnuts to the line so they are all hanging down at the same height. On the count of three, everyone has to start eating their doughnut...without using their hands! The first person to finish their doughnut is the winner.

Top tip
This game can get messy so make sure you cover the floor with old newspaper or play it outside!

Do you dare?

Give everyone a few strips of paper and ask them to write a dare on each one. Fold them up and put them in a bowl. Take it in turns to pull a dare out of the bowl and read it aloud. You must then do the dare you've chosen or get a penalty point. The person with the fewest penalty points, once the bowl is empty, is the winner.

Top tip
Try to think of funny dares that your friends won't be too embarrassed to do.

Drawing in the dark

Give everyone a piece of paper and a pen. Put blindfolds on and try to draw a picture of me. When everyone's finished, take your blindfolds off and look at the pictures. The person whose drawing looks most like me is the winner.

Top tip
Make sure you spread old newspaper under your pieces of paper so you don't make a mess!

Memory Test

One person collects 10 different objects from around the house. The other players have 10 seconds to look at the objects and try to memorise them. The objects are then removed and each player is given one minute to list as many of the objects as they can remember. The player who remembers the most is the winner. Play again with a different person collecting 10 different objects.

Top tip
Add another object each time you play to make the game harder.

Celebrity bingo

Each player makes a bingo card by drawing a large square onto a piece of paper and dividing it into nine smaller squares. Cut pictures of 12 different celebrities out of a magazine. Write the names of nine of the celebrities onto the squares on your bingo card. Place the pictures face down and take it in turns to turn one over. If you have that celebrity on your bingo card, cross it out. The winner is the first player to cross out all of their celebrity names and shout 'bingo'.

Top tip
You could use characters from your favourite TV show instead of celebrities.

Places to go

Whatever the weather, there's always somewhere fun to go with friends!

I can't think of any indoor game that is more fun than bowling! Who doesn't enjoy knocking down those pins? And even if you're not very good, you can still have a giggle at all the balls rolling down the gutter! Why not wear the same colour tops when you go with friends so you look like a team.

Bowling alley

Beach

If you live near the coast, a sunny day at the seaside with friends is so much fun! You can splash in the sea, eat ice creams and top up your tan (don't forget the sun screen!). And if you're too old for building sandcastles, why not make a sand sculpture instead?

Ice-skating rink

Ice-skating with friends is so much fun. If, like me, you're a bit wobbly on the ice, having someone to hold on to makes all the difference!

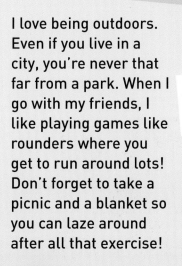

Park

I love being outdoors. Even if you live in a city, you're never that far from a park. When I go with my friends, I like playing games like rounders where you get to run around lots! Don't forget to take a picnic and a blanket so you can laze around after all that exercise!

Going to the cinema is such fun! My friends and I spend ages reading reviews before we decide what to watch. And, of course, you can't watch a movie without stocking up on some yummy snacks first!

Shopping centre

Clothes shopping with friends is one of my favourite hobbies! It's great to get honest opinions about what suits you and have help deciding what to buy. I also love seeing what everyone else tries on – it's like having my own personal fashion show in the changing rooms!

See who can scream the loudest as you ride the rollercoaster, get wet on the log flume and spin around on the big wheel! Even if you don't like the scary rides, there are plenty of other things to keep you entertained. The carousel is my favourite!

Art gallery

If you're lucky enough to live near an art gallery, don't dismiss it because you think it's boring. Exhibitions can be fun, vibrant and full of life! Look up what's on and choose one that sounds interesting. Visit with a small group of friends – galleries are quiet places!

Party planning

Choosing a theme

Themed parties are great fun and make an event really special. Choose a theme that can be reflected in your food, decorations and games. Some of my favourite themes are:
- Colours (pink of course!)
- Under the sea
- Places (choose a well-known country or city)
- Tropical paradise
- Space

Don't wait for your birthday, you can throw a party for friends any time of the year!

Invitations

Making your own invitations adds a lovely personal touch to your party. Use your imagination and try to do something a little bit different. You could write on balloons which your guests have to blow up to read or bake cookies to give with your invites.

Decorations

If you can decorate the space where your party will take place, it will really bring the event to life. Choose decorations that go with your theme and make as many as you can – your friends will appreciate that much more than shop bought decorations!

Games

Party games are lots of fun and will keep your guests amused for hours. See pages 28-31 for some ideas or search for 'party games' on the internet. If you can play games that relate to your theme, even better! Buy some sweets or small gifts to give out as prizes for the winners.

Food and drink

Ask your mama or papa to help you write a shopping list of food and drink for your party. The easiest party food is things that your guests can help themselves to like sandwiches and cakes. Prepare your food in advance so you aren't cooking when the party's in full swing – you don't want to miss out on all the fun!

Music

A party wouldn't be a party without music! If you have an Mp3 player, make a playlist of your favourite songs and leave it running on the day. If you're using CDs, put them in the order you want to play them so you can switch quickly as each one ends.

Goody bags

I love coming away from a party with a little goody bag full of surprises! They don't have to be expensive to put together and will make the excitement of your party last a little bit longer. You could include things like sweets, balloons, streamers and jokes written on pretty paper.

Tidying up

Clean up as soon as your last guest has left. If you put everything back to the way it was before, your mama and papa are more likely to let you have another party!

Party to-do list

Tick each item off as you do it!

- ♡ Ask mama and papa's permission
- ♡ Decide on a date and time
- ♡ Choose a theme
- ♡ Make invitations
- ♡ Send invitations
- ♡ Make decorations
- ♡ Choose games to play
- ♡ Buy prizes for winners
- ♡ Write a shopping list for food and drink
- ♡ Buy food and drink
- ♡ Prepare food
- ♡ Choose music
- ♡ Make goody bags
- ♡ Tidy up

Sleepovers

There are a few extra things you need to think about when planning a sleepover. Use my checklist on page 43 to make sure you don't forget anything! Always check your plans with your mama and papa.

Where to sleep

Work out the best room in which to have your sleepover, then plan where everyone will sleep. Do you have enough beds, sofas or inflatable mattresses for everyone? Will anyone have to sleep on the floor?

Midnight feast

A midnight feast is lots of fun at any time! Check what time you're allowed to stay up until and start your midnight feast a few hours before bedtime – it's no fun going to bed with a full tummy!

Fab friends

Make a list of fun friends and check how many guests you are allowed to invite before you begin planning your sleepover.

Bedding

Make sure you have enough duvets and pillows for all of your guests. If you don't, ask your friends to bring their own.

Lights out

Keep quiet late at night. Remember, other people in the house might want to sleep even if you don't!

Movies

My favourite sleepover activity is watching a movie tucked up in bed! Choose a film that you know your friends will enjoy and make sure everyone is nice and comfortable before you begin!

Breakfast

Plan a breakfast menu. You could have something simple like toast or cereal or something a bit more special like pancakes or crumpets. Make sure you help to clear up afterwards!

Getting ready

With so many people wanting to get ready at the same time, you may have to make a bathroom rota! Check the best time slot with everyone else in the house to avoid a queue!

Sleepover checklist

Tick each item off as you do it!

- ♡ Ask mama and papa's permission
- ♡ Choose guests
- ♡ Decide where everyone will sleep
- ♡ Sort out bedding
- ♡ Choose movie
- ♡ Prepare midnight feast
- ♡ Keep quiet late at night
- ♡ Plan breakfast menu
- ♡ Clear up after breakfast
- ♡ Write bathroom rota
- ♡ Tidy up

Tidying up

Once you're all up and dressed, make sure you tidy away all the bedding and put the room back to the way it was before. Don't forget to open the window to let in a bit of fresh air!

Guide to Friendship

Things to Make

Presents for friends

It's lovely to receive an unexpected gift. Here are a few things you could make for your friends.

Photo frame

It's easy to decorate a plain wooden phot
frame and turn it into a special present fo
a friend. You could paint it and add
glitter and sequins, stick on dried
flowers or glue on a pretty ribbon.
Don't forget to put a photo
of you and your friend
inside before you
give your gift!

Memory box

A memory box is a place to keep
things that remind you of special
times, such as tickets to events you
really enjoyed, invitations for parties
and keepsakes from fun days out. It's
easy to make a memory box from an
empty shoebox. Simply cover the
box with pretty wrapping paper
and decorate it with
photographs, pictures
from magazines
or stickers.

Friendship card

It's easy to forget to tell friends how much they mean to you. Why not make and send a friendship card to show that you care? Take a plain piece of card and fold it in half. Decorate the front and write a message inside telling your friend why they're so great!

Writing paper

Using pretty writing paper is such a treat! It's easy to transform a piece of plain writing paper into something really special. You could add a glitter border, draw pretty flowers in the corners or make it smell gorgeous with a little squirt of your favourite perfume. Decorate a few sheets then wrap a ribbon around them before giving to your friend.

Photo collage

I love being surrounded by photos of my friends! A collage is the perfect way to display lots of pictures of you having fun together.

You will need:
Scissors
Glue
A picture frame
A piece of cardboard

Younger Hello Kitty fans: always ask mama or papa for help.

Taking new pics

If you don't have enough photos or you don't want to use the ones you already have, take some more especially for your collage. You can turn this into a fun event in itself! Make sure your friends have plenty of outfits to change into so it doesn't look like all the photos were taken on the same day and include lots of props such as food and magazines. Don't forget that you should be in some of the photos too!

Choosing your pics

You will need lots of photos to make your collage so dig as many out as you can. You'll need to cut them up so you may want to make copies and keep the originals in one piece. Make sure you have a nice mixture of close-ups and long shots with interesting backgrounds

Finding a frame

Your collage can be whatever size you choose, but I think the bigger the better! Decide where you want to hang your collage and choose a frame that will fit in the space. A plain frame will look very arty or you could choose one with a pattern for a more fun look. Look in homeware shops or on the internet, or, if you want something a bit different, check out charity shops and second hand furniture stores.

Younger Hello Kitty fans: ask mama or papa to help you hang your collage.

Cutting and sticking

Once you've got your photographs and your frame, the fun can begin! Cut around the edge of your chosen photos, following the outlines of your friends, or cut your pictures into different shapes. Then stick them onto a piece of cardboard the same size as your frame – you can overlap them or leave spaces between the pictures. There really aren't any rules to collage making – just try things out and go with what looks good to you. Once you're happy, mount your collage in the frame and hang it on your wall.

Time capsule

Make a lasting reminder of your friendship to open up in years to come!

How it works

A time capsule is a container that you place items inside. It is then hidden or buried for a long time and opened up on an agreed date.

The container

Choose a strong container that is airtight so your items will last – a plastic box will be perfect. Make sure the lid fits tightly and clips into place. If you are going to bury your time capsule, the container will need to be waterproof too.

The contents

Choose items that represent your friendship and show life as it is today. You could include a newspaper, your favourite book, a gift from a friend, a CD, a TV guide, photographs of you and your friends, a shopping receipt, a stamp, a magazine, a clothes catalogue, letters, postcards, some coins and some food packaging (don't include food though, you don't want anything that will go off over the years!).

xoxo xoxo

The agreement

You and your friends must all agree when the time capsule will be opened. Will it be in three years' time? Five years? 10 years? Write your agreed date down and make sure everyone has a copy. Nobody must open the time capsule before that date.

Where to keep it

Traditionally, time capsules are buried outside but it might be easier to hide yours away in your house. It needs to be a place that people don't go to very often – an attic, cellar or storage cupboard would be ideal. Make sure you label your time capsule with your friends' names and the date it is to be opened in case you forget what it is!

The opening

On your agreed date, you must all gather together to open your time capsule. The longer you leave it, the more interesting the objects inside will seem!

Younger Hello Kitty fans: ask mama or papa before you hide your time capsule.

Friendship scrapbook

A scrapbook is a great way of recording all the fun things that you and your friends do together.

Choose a nice big scrap book with plenty of pages.

Personalise the front cover with a fun photo of you and your friends.

When you see a really good film, keep the cinema ticket and stick it inside. You can do the same with tickets for other events and occasions.

ADMIT ONE

Stick some of your favourite photos inside – remember to write who everyone is and what they're doing in the pictures.

Ask your friends to write messages to you on one of the pages inside.

Write your friends'
details inside. You
could include their
names, ages, where they
live, their favourite TV
programmes, their favourite
colours and the reasons why
they're your friends.

Save invitations from fun
birthday parties and stick
them inside. You could also
write notes to remind you
what you wore to the party,
what games you played
and what you bought your
friend as a present.

Keep birthday and Christmas
cards from your friends and stick
your favourite ones inside.

Cooking

Pizza muffins

These simple pizzas make perfect party food. Best of all, they're so easy to make!

Ingredients

* Muffins
* Tomato puree
* Cheddar cheese (grated)
* Mixed dried herbs

Toppings such as:
* Cherry tomatoes
* Olives
* Mushrooms
* Onions
* Salami
* Peppers
* Ham
* Pineapple

Younger Hello Kitty fans: always ask mama or papa to help you.

How to make

1. Carefully cut a muffin in half and toast both pieces in a toaster.

2. Allow the muffin halves to cool before spreading with tomato puree

3. Sprinkle with grated cheese and add your chosen toppings.

4. Cook in the oven at 190°C/375°F/Gas mark 5 for 10 minutes or until the cheese has melted and the toppings are warm.

Top tip

Put different toppings on each muffin half for twice the fun!

Gingerbread cookies

Cooking with friends is lots of fun! Follow this recipe for delicious, easy to make gingerbread cookies.

Ingredients

- ✶ 340g plain flour (sifted)
- ✶ 115g butter or margarine (softened)
- ✶ 100g soft brown sugar
- ✶ 190g golden syrup
- ✶ 2 teaspoons ground ginger
- ✶ 1 teaspoon bicarbonate of soda

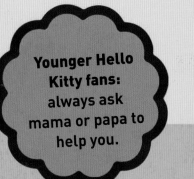

Younger Hello Kitty fans: always ask mama or papa to help you.

How to make

 1. Preheat the oven to 190°C/375°F/Gas mark 5, but check with mama or papa first.

 2. In a bowl, beat the sugar and butter/margarine together until light and creamy. You can use an electric whisk if you have one or a wooden spoon.

 3. Stir in the golden syrup, sifted flour, ginger and bicarbonate of soda.

 4. Knead the mixture into a smooth dough using your hands.

 5. Refrigerate the dough for 10 minutes or until firm.

 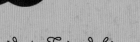

Roll the dough out between two sheets of cling film or baking paper (don't use a floured surface) until about 4mm thick.

Cut the dough into shapes using a cookie cutter or blunt knife.

Place your cookies onto a non-stick baking tray and cook for 8-10 minutes until golden brown.

Let your cookies cool on a wire rack before eating.

Top Tip

Once your cookies have cooled, you could decorate them with icing or melted chocolate.

Fruit kebabs

Use your favourite fruits to make this delicious, colourful treat.

Younger Hello Kitty fans: always ask mama or papa to help you.

Ingredients

Four different types of fruit such as:
* Banana
* Strawberries
* Kiwi
* Apple
* Orange
* Grapes
* Mango
* Pineapple
* Marshmallows

How to make

1. Wash your chosen fruit and peel if necessary.

2. Carefully cut your fruit into chunky pieces.

3. Thread the fruit pieces and marshmallows on wooden skewers.

4. Cover the kebabs and chill for an hour before eating.

Top Tip

Fruit kebabs are even more delicious when dipped in Greek yoghurt, honey or melted chocolate and rolled in chopped mixed nuts.

Cupcakes

The best thing about making cupcakes is decorating them! Try to make yours as unique as you can.

Ingredients

For 12 cupcakes:
* 125g butter (softened)
* 125g caster sugar
* 2 eggs (lightly beaten)
* 1 tsp vanilla extract
* 125g self-raising flour
* 2 tbsp milk

How to make

1. Preheat the oven to 190°C/375°F/Gas mark 5.
2. Line a 12-hole bun tin with paper cases.
3. In a bowl, beat the butter and sugar together until pale and fluffy. Use an electric whisk or a wooden spoon.
4. Add the beaten egg a little at a time, then beat in the vanilla extract.

Younger Hello Kitty fans: always ask mama or papa to help you.

5 Sift in half the flour and fold into the mixture. Add the milk and the rest of the flour and fold until the mixture has combined.

6 Spoon the mixture into the bun cases.

7 Bake for 12 minutes or until the cupcakes have risen and are golden brown.

8 Let the cupcakes cool for 10 minutes before removing from the bun tin. Leave them on a wire rack until they are completely cool.

Decorating ideas

★ Icing
★ Chocolate spread
★ Sifted icing sugar
★ Strawberries
★ Jelly sweets
★ Chocolate drops
★ Coconut
★ Jam
★ Cherries

Clubs and Hobbies

Start your own club

Setting up your very own club is such a fun thing to do. Make sure you get all your friends involved.

Choose your theme

First of all you must decide what your club is going to be about. It could be dedicated to a certain hobby, such as ice-skating or cooking, or it could be about something more abstract, like the colour pink or making people laugh. Choose something that will provide lots of fun and make sure your friends will be interested in it too – it's no fun being in a club on your own!

Pick a name

Every club needs a name. Yours should be fun, catchy and easy to remember. If you can't decide, come up with a list of ideas and ask a friend to help you choose which one to use.

Recruit your members

Is your club going to be for close friends only or are you going to use it as a way to make new friends? Will it be open to anyone who wants to join or will you have a limit on numbers? Once you've decided who you'd like to be in your club, send them an invite to the first meeting.

Choose a clubhouse

Now you know how many people are coming, you must decide where your club will meet. Make sure you choose somewhere with enough room for everyone and try to make it as comfortable as possible. Remember to ask your mama and papa's permission if you want to meet in your house or garden or tell them where you'll be if your club will meet somewhere else.

Your first club meeting

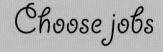

Write the rules

Now you have a club with members, it's important that everyone feels equal so it's time to come up with a list of club rules. Let everyone have their say and try to find a compromise if you don't all agree!

Choose jobs

You might be the founding member, but it's nice if everyone in the club can have a job to do. Try to match your friends' skills to the job – if someone is good with money, they can be the Treasurer. Other roles could include President, Secretary and Head of Communications.

Make badges

Every good club has a logo. Try to come up with something eye-catching that shows what your club is all about. Once you've designed your logo, make club badges for everyone. As well as the logo, you could add names and club roles.

Plan ahead

The best thing about being in a club is having lots of fun things to do. Write a big long list of ideas for future meetings. You could include things to make, places to visit and games to play. Cross each thing off the list as you do it and add something else so your list never ends!

Try something new

Listen to a type of music you've never heard before – do you know any jazz, classical or opera?

Learn a language – even if it's only a few simple sentences.

Walk a different route to school or the shops – a change is as good as a holiday!

Try some food from a country you've never been to – you can find Thai, Indian and Mexican food in most supermarkets.

Learn how to knit – making a simple scarf isn't as hard as it looks!

Trace your family history – it's so interesting to discover your roots and the internet has made it easier than ever.

Play a new sport – have you ever tried baseball, basketball or cricket?

Take a class – it could be in dance, sewing or Spanish...choose anything that interests you.

Learn how to play an instrument – even if it's only one simple song.

Style your hair differently – a new look can make you feel like a new you!

Share your skills

You and your friends must have lots of skills between you. Think about what you're all good at and see if you can share your talents out!

Singing

Is there someone in your group of friends who can hold a tune? If so, ask her to give the rest of you a singing lesson. You might not end up a superstar, but you'll have lots of fun trying!

Dancing

Some people are natural dancers. If a friend knows how to move, ask her to share her secrets with you. You could even make up a routine together.

Writing

Whether it is stories, poems or letters, good writers know how to bring words to life. Ask your writer friend to share her skills and help you pen a fabulous story.

Cooking

Do you have a friend who knows how to make delicious cupcakes or mouth-watering cookies? If so, ask her to show you how it's done. She'll probably enjoy showing off her talents in the kitchen!

Planning

Some people are super organised and make everything look easy. If you have a planner as a friend, ask her to help you plan your next party...and give you some organisational tips along the way.

Sports

Is one of your friends good at a particular sport? Ask her to give you some pointers to improve your game.

Beauty

Make your own face masks

You and your friends can have lots of fun experimenting with beauty routines. Try making these yummy face masks at your next sleepover.

Avocado and honey moisturiser

You will need

* ½ avocado
* 1 tbsp honey

Preparation

Mash the avocado in a bowl until creamy and stir in the honey. Apply to freshly washed skin and leave for 10 minutes. Wipe off with a cool cloth.

Great for

dry skin

Apple refresher
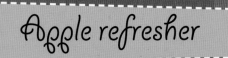

You will need

★ 1 apple (grated)
★ 5 tbsp honey (warmed)

Preparation

Stir all the ingredients together and apply to freshly cleansed skin. Leave for 10 minutes then wash off with warm water.

Great for

oily skin

Banana and avocado smoother

Great for

combination skin

You will need

★ ½ banana
★ ½ avocado
★ 2 tbsp natural yogurt
★ 1 tsp olive oil

Preparation

Purée all of the ingredients using a blender. Apply to clean skin and leave for 15 minutes. Rinse off with warm water.

Makeovers

Giving my friends makeovers is one of my favourite activities! Make sure you allow plenty of time for the transformation!

Begin your makeover with a beauty treatment such as a face mask (see pages 76-77 to make your own). It's lovely to be pampered!

Give your friend a whole new look – if she normally wears her hair loose, try putting it up. If she wear pink lipgloss, give her red instead!

Take 'before' and 'after' photos so you can see what a difference you've made.

Look through magazines for hairstyles that you like and try to copy them. Don't worry if they don't look exactly the same!

Experiment with hair accessories such as Alice bands, bows and clips.

If you and your friends are all having makeovers, try to make everyone look completely different – one of you could have your hair straightened, one can be curled and one can go for loose waves.

Don't forget the finishing touches like nail varnish. You could choose a colour that matches your friend's outfit or go with one that clashes dramatically.

If your makeover includes make-up, don't forget to wash it off properly before going to bed – skin needs to be able to breathe while you sleep.

Heavenly hair treatments

Have a pampering session with your friends and try one of these treatments to give your hair a new lease of life.

Deep treat

You will need

* Your usual conditioner
* A plastic shower cap
* A comb

Directions

Wash your hair as normal, then towel dry. Smooth in a big dollop of conditioner and comb it through. Cover your hair with a plastic shower cap. Leave for at least three hours before rinsing the conditioner out. For best results, leave overnight.

Great for **moisturising dry hair**

Silky smooth

You will need

* 1 tsp olive oil
* 1 egg yolk
* 1 cup water

Directions

Beat the egg yolk until frothy and add the olive oil. Beat again until the mixture has combined. Stir in the water. Massage into your scalp and through your hair. Leave for 10 minutes before rinsing thoroughly.

Great for

taming flyaway hair

Green dream

You will need

★ 3 tbsp mayonnaise
★ ½ avocado

Great for

livening up dull hair

Directions

Mash the avocado in a bowl until it makes a smooth paste. Stir in the mayonnaise. Smooth into your hair and cover with a shower cap. Leave for 20 minutes before rinsing out.

Super shine

You will need

★ The juice of one lemon
★ 500ml warm water

Directions

Wash and condition your hair as normal. Add the lemon juice to the hot water and pour over your hair. Do not rinse out.

Great for **making hair shine**

Pampering day

One of my favourite beauty treats is organising a pampering day for my friends. It's so relaxing!

Choose a day when you don't have anything else planned so you can take your time – a day during the weekend or school holidays is perfect and check with mama and papa.

Decide on the treatments you'd like to have and plan your day.

Pampering days should be relaxing so choose some nice, soothing music to play in the background.

Wear something comfortable and that you don't mind getting dirty, like loose trousers and an old T-shirt.

Make sure you have enough space to do the treatments you've chosen and enough hot water if necessary.

Make sure you have enough clean towels for everyone or ask your friends to bring their own.

Prepare some healthy snacks to enjoy between treatments.

Ideas for treatments

- 🤍 Face mask (see pages 76-77 for how to make your own)
- 🤍 Manicure
- 🤍 Pedicure
- 🤍 Foot scrub
- 🤍 Nail painting
- 🤍 Hair treatment (see pages 80-81 for how to make your own)
- 🤍 Hair styling

Fashion

Planning a clothes swapping party

When you get bored of your clothes don't throw them away, swap them for something else instead!

To make a clothes swapping party successful, you will need at least four guests, but the more the better. Invite as many as you can fit in!

Ask your guests to bring along any clothes, shoes, bags or accessories that they no longer wear but are still in good condition.

If you have space to hang the clothes up it will be easier for people to look through them.

Sort the items into sections so it's easier for people to look through them. Put all the tops together, all the jeans together and so on.

Label each item with a number – you could use raffle tickets or make your own labels.

Give your guests a set time to look through all the items and write down what they'd like. If more than one person wants the same thing, draw the name out of a hat.

To keep things fair, give everyone a ticket for each item they donate which they can swap for a new item.

If you have any unwanted items left at the end of your party, donate them to your local charity shop.

Make sure you have plenty of mirrors so your guests can see what they look like.

If you have the space, create a changing room where people can try things on.

Don't forget to ask mama and papa's permission before planning your clothes swapping party. And don't swap anything without checking with them first.

Style your friends

All the top celebrities have a stylist to help them choose what to wear, so why shouldn't you?

Choose a friend who you trust and take it in turns to style each other.

Pretend your friend is going to an event such as a ball or movie premiere. What you choose will have to fit the occasion.

Don't let your friend look in a mirror until you have completely finished!

Choose shoes that will match your friend's outfit. Get her to try lots of different styles – sometimes the most unexpected things look good together.

Look through your friend's wardrobe and pull out any suitable items of clothing.

The right accessories can make an outfit. Don't be afraid to experiment with different colours and styles until you are happy with the look.

Mix and match and try lots of different combinations until you're sure you have the best look.

Photoshoot fun!

Now you and your friends are looking good, it's time to plan your first photoshoot!

Location, location, location!

Choose a location that offers variety – a house with a garden is ideal. Don't forget to ask mama and papa's permission first!

Choosing your clothes

Make sure you have plenty of different outfits in various styles. Bring along lots of accessories too! Make sure you have somewhere private where the models can change!

Shooting your photoshoot

Using a digital camera is best for photoshoots, then you can check your pics as you go. Take it in turns to be the photographer and the model – both roles are lots of fun!

Strike a pose!

Have a fashion magazine to hand so you can copy models' poses if you don't know what to do. Have fun with it and be as silly as you like!

Make it varied

Aim for a variety of shots in different locations (this could be different rooms in a house or, if you're limited to one room, different places in the room).

Types of pics

Experiment with close-up and distant shots, and landscape and portrait pics. Take as many as you like – you can always delete some later!

Using props

Props are a great way to bring a photoshoot to life. You could use food, magazines, books... or anything else you can get your hands on.

The next stage

Don't forget to print your favourite pics from your photoshoot. You could even use them to make your own fashion magazine!

Customising your clothes

Customising is a great way to add new life to old clothes. Plus, you'll end up with some thing that's unique.

Invite a few friends round to help – it's great to get other people's ideas.

Choose old clothes or buy an inexpensive, plain T-shirt especially for customising. Don't forget to ask mama or papa's permission before you begin!

You might choose to customise a bag, a belt or a hat instead of clothes.

Ask everyone to bring some materials so you have plenty of choice. Sequins, beads, ribbon, buttons, material scraps, fabric pens, feathers and lace are all great for customising.

Look through fashion magazines or catalogues to get ideas.

Have scissors, glue and a needle and thread handy. Make sure mama and papa know if you'll be cutting or sewing.

Lay out your chosen design on your clothes to see what it will look like before you start sticking or sewing – make sure you're happy with it before you begin.

Be careful when washing your customised item for the first time – you don't want to ruin all your hard work by spinning it for too long!

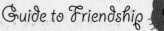

Secrets

Keeping secrets

A true friend will trust you to keep her secrets. Make sure that you do!

A secret is a very special thing between friends – if your friend confides in you, it means she trusts you.

Never laugh at a friend's secret – you don't want to make her feel silly.

If you write any secrets down, don't leave them where someone else might find them (unless they are written in code, of course!).

Secrets should be harmless. If you feel a friend's secret is hurting her or others, tell a grown-up who you trust.

If your friend's secrets are harmless, never ever tell them to anyone without her permission.

Having a secret can be fun but make sure your other friends don't feel left out because of it.

Sharing secrets

Only share your secrets with friends you can trust.

You could invent a secret code that only you and your friends have the key for. Then you can write each other messages that nobody else will understand!

A secret doesn't have to be big, it could be tiny thing such as liking a TV programm that everyone else thinks is rubbish!

Don't ever feel like you have to share your secrets. If you want to keep something to yourself, then that's just fine.

Remember, once you've shared a secret, you can't take it back so be absolutely certain you don't mind your friend knowing before you tell.

You could keep a secret diary that only you and your friends are allowed to write in. Take it in turns to hide the diary somewhere safe.

Secrets box

A secrets box is the perfect place for storing all your secrets!

You will need

* An empty box with a lid
* Pretty wrapping paper
* Scissors
* Glue or sticky tape

1

Carefully wrap your box and lid in wrapping paper and stick in place.

2

Decide what you will put in your secrets box. It could be photographs you don't want anyone else to see, private notes from friends or wishes written on pieces of paper.

3

Find a good hiding place for your secrets box. Choose somewhere handy so you can look through the box whenever you want to.

Hello Kitty's secrets...

Secret signs

It is lots of fun to invent secret greetings and symbols to use with your very best friends!

Invent a special handshake to use as a greeting – make it complicated so nobody else can copy you!

Make up your own secret language – you could try talking backwards or swapping words around!

Give each other nicknames but don't tell anyone else what they mean!

Use different colours to say different things – wearing something red could mean I have a secret to tell you!

Write messages using a secret code – you could invent your own or use the one below.

Secret Code

Use this secret code to write messages to your friends.

A	B	C	D	E
F	G	H	I	J
K	L	M	N	O
P	Q	R	S	T
U	V	W	X	Y	Z

Old and New friends

Meeting new friends

You never know when you might make a new friend, that's what makes it so exciting!

The new girl

If someone new starts at your school, be as nice as possible and try to include them in things you do. Being the new girl can be scary so having someone friendly by your side can make all the difference.

A common interest

Clubs are great places to make new friends because you'll already have something in common! Check out the after school or weekend clubs in your area and choose one that sounds like fun.

Flash that smile!

Nobody wants to make friends with someone who's miserable so make sure you smile when you meet new people!

Take your time

Try to be open when you meet new people and give them a chance. Even if you don't warm to someone straightaway it doesn't mean they won't be a great friend once you get to know them.

Overcoming shyness

Sometimes it can be hard to start talking to people you don't know. If you feel a bit shy, take a friend with you. Things are always easier when there are two of you.

Different is good!

Remember, friends don't have to be exactly the same as you. It's nice to have some things in common but it's good to have differences too.

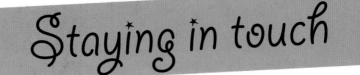

Staying in touch

Long distance friendships can work, you just have to try a little bit harder.

If a good friend is moving away, it doesn't have to be the end of your friendship...as long as you both make an effort to keep in touch.

Remember, friends don't have to live around the corner. It's fun to have friends in different towns and even different countries!

Email is a great way to let your friend know what you've been up to. It's quick and easy and they'll receive your message straightaway.

Receiving letters in the post is such a treat! Make your letter special by decorating the writing paper and envelope with stickers, drawings or photographs.

Don't forget to phone your friend when you can. It's always nice to hear a familiar voice. Ask mama and papa's permission first.

If you get a new haircut or buy a new outfit, post or email a photograph of you to your friend. Ask her to do the same so you keep up-to-date with any new looks.

If you don't have time to write a long letter, send your friend a postcard instead.

If it's possible, try to arrange to meet your long distance friend as regularly as you can. Ask your mama and papa to help you with arrangements.

Making up

Make up as soon after a falling out as you can – the longer you leave it, the harder it will be.

Talk through what went wrong and how it made you both feel.

Don't be afraid to make the first move – even if you think it wasn't your fault!

Try to see things from the other person's point of view – they might see what happened completely differently to you.

Think of ways to stop the same thing happening again.

Once you've sorted out your differences, do something fun together, like watching your favourite movie.

Growing together
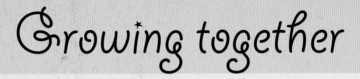

As you and your friends grow up, things may change, but make sure you grow together rather than growing apart.

Make time for each other
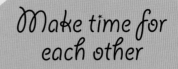

You may not always be in the same class or even the same school as your friend but that doesn't mean you have to stop being friends. Just make more of an effort to see each other after school and at weekends.

Change is good!

As you grow up you may develop different interests from your friend. Think of this as a good thing – it will give you something else to talk about!

Show an interest

If your friend takes up a new hobby try to show an interest in it, even it if isn't something you'd want to do yourself.

Magical memories

Take time to remember the fun things you've shared together. Looking back through old photos is a great place to start.

Keep a record

Write a list of why you are friends and look back at it from time to time – it's great to be reminded of the best things about your friend!

Ask advice

Talk to your mama or papa about their friends. Are they still in touch with people they knew at your age? Ask them for advice on staying friends forever.

Friendship Tips

How to be a better friend

Even great friends sometimes have room for improvement! Everyday I try my hardest to be the best friend I can be.

Make time for your friend even when you're busy. You don't have to spend a whole day together to show her that you care, sometimes a 10 minute chat will do.

Never take your friend for granted. You're lucky to have her, just as she's lucky to have you.

Try to tune into how she's feeling. If she's a bit sad she might need cheering up, if she's fed up she may appreciate having a good moan and if she's happy she probably just wants someone to laugh along with her.

Try not to get jealous of her other friends – if she's so great, of course other people want to be her friend too!

Make her feel special – surprise her with a homemade gift to show her that you care.

Listen to your friend and remember the things that are important to her. It's a lovely feeling when someone knows you almost as well as you know yourself.

Sharing

It's great to have a friend you can share things with, whether it's shoes, cookies or memories!

If you and a friend wear the same size clothes, it's nice to borrow something from them every now and then. Especially if the item is completely different to anything you own!

If you borrow something from a friend, take good care of it and always remember to give it back.

Little gestures, such as sharing your chocolate bar with your friend at break time, can mean as much as the big things.

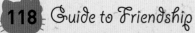

Remember, sharing works both ways. Don't expect your friend to share with you if you won't share with her!

No matter how often you share things, always ask a friend before borrowing something of hers.

Shared memories are one of the nicest things about friendship. Make sure you take the time to talk about fun things you've done together so you'll always remember them.

Friendship rules

My friends and I came up with these friendship rules to make sure we stay friends forever!

Never gossip about a friend behind her back.

2

Always make up after an argument.

3

Always keep in touch – even if you don't live close to each other.

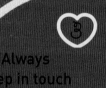

♥ 4 Be prepared to share your food, clothes and time!

♥ 5 Remember, friends always come before boys!

♥ 6 Never forget a friend's birthday.

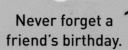

♥ 7 Never tell a friend's secrets.

♥ 8 Always be honest with your friend.

♥ 9 Don't forget to tell your friend how much she means to you.

♥ 10 Promise to stay friends forever!

Guide to Friendship **121**

Hello Kitty says...

"Good friends are for life."

"You can never have too many friends."

Goodbye!

I hope you've enjoyed reading this book and have learnt lots of things about friendship. Friends are great and you're lucky to have them in your life!

I've given you loads of ideas for exciting things to do with friends and I'm sure you can come up with plenty more yourself. Whatever you end up doing, make sure you have lots and lots of fun!

Give your friends a big hug from me!

Lots of love,

Hello Kitty

x